BE A HERO!

BE A HERO!

THE HANDBOOK FOR MEN

EVELYN CROSS

Copyright © 2022 Evelyn Cross.

All rights reserved. No part of this book may be used or reproduced by any means, graphic, electronic, or mechanical, including photocopying, recording, taping or by any information storage retrieval system without the written permission of the author except in the case of brief quotations embodied in critical articles and reviews.

Archway Publishing books may be ordered through booksellers or by contacting:

Archway Publishing
1663 Liberty Drive
Bloomington, IN 47403
www.archwaypublishing.com
844-669-3957

Because of the dynamic nature of the Internet, any web addresses or links contained in this book may have changed since publication and may no longer be valid. The views expressed in this work are solely those of the author and do not necessarily reflect the views of the publisher, and the publisher hereby disclaims any responsibility for them.

Any people depicted in stock imagery provided by Getty Images are models, and such images are being used for illustrative purposes only. Certain stock imagery © Getty Images.

Scripture quotations are taken from the New American Bible, revised edition © 2010, 1991, 1986, 1970 Confraternity of Christian Doctrine, Washington, D.C. and are used by permission of the copyright owner. All Rights Reserved.

ISBN: 978-1-6657-2488-3 (sc)
ISBN: 978-1-6657-2489-0 (e)

Library of Congress Control Number: 2022910678

Print information available on the last page.

Archway Publishing rev. date: 7/13/2022

PREFACE

My mother loved magazines. Thick glossy paper, bright colors, and photos on every page. A child of "The Great Depression", she "pinched pennies" and "made dollars stretch". Trips to the grocery store required a list. List in hand, she did her "value shopping". She saved a penny here, and a penny there, on each item. She arrived at the check-out with pennies in hand to select a magazine from the rack. "Ladies' Home Journal" and "Good Housekeeping" were among American homemakers' favorites. Every issue contained family-pleasing recipes. There were a variety of articles. From gardening to food preservation. From decorating to house-cleaning tips, and honing organizational skills. Sewing, knitting, crocheting, and quilting projects were featured. The homemaker's goal was to provide a high standard of living for her household, while making her husband's paycheck stretch. There were articles teaching mothers how to raise children. And articles begging the question, "Can This Marriage be Saved?"

I was a "Baby Boomer", the generation born following World War II. America, at long last, had money to spend. We spent our money on new homes, new cars, and better educations. We bought giant photo magazines to display on our coffee tables. Professional journals, and "National Geographic" arrived in the mail. Men's magazines appealed to hobby, and sports enthusiasts. The "Sports Illustrated Swimsuit Issue" was an all-time favorite. Later, "Playboy" introduced a "mainstream", and "socially acceptable", sex-topic publication. Pornography hid under the American mattress.

By the 1970's, I was raising children of my own. "Ebony Magazine" graced our coffee table. Before the "world" chimed in to discourage my mixed-race children, I wanted them to know that they looked forward to a lifetime of opportunities. To encourage their enthusiasm for reading and learning, I ordered gift subscriptions to children's magazines, of their very own. They received "Highlights for Children" and "Ranger Rick". A child gets excited when mail arrives with his name on it. Sometimes we read the magazines, and worked on the projects together, as a family. Like my mother, I "pinched pennies" and "value shopped" at the grocery store. I bought the "National Enquirer" for myself, at checkout. You never know when you will be kidnapped by aliens, outside in the backyard, hanging laundry. By the 1990's "Men in Black" debuted at the "box office", to solve this problem.

One day, at the magazine rack, a deafening silence fell. Where were the male counterparts to "Ladies' Home Journal"? Or, "Good Housekeeping"? Due to the effectiveness of "Women's Liberation", "Working Mother" now appeared on the rack. There were magazines aplenty, supporting women in their homemaker roles. Magazines aplenty purported to help women become better wives, mothers, and homemakers. Where were the magazines supporting men in their efforts to become better husbands and fathers? Where were the "how to's"? How to build and maintain a family home? How best to provide for your family? How to protect your loved ones? Don't men need to understand the dynamics of family relationships? Don't men benefit by learning effective communication skills? And parenting skills? Where was "Working Father" magazine? Doesn't every husband hope to enjoy a happy marriage? Doesn't every father hope to provide his family with a secure, and stable home? Doesn't every father want his children "to turn out well"? Good men deserve our support. Good husbands and fathers are heroes. This book was written to support our heroes!

CONTENTS

Chapter 1 My Dad 1

Chapter 2 Our Father 8

Chapter 3 My Hero 13

Chapter 4 Soar With Eagles 20

Chapter 5 "Truth, Justice, and the American Way" 25

Chapter 6 Heroes Save Lives 31

Chapter 7 Calling All Heroes! 37

Chapter 8 THINK! 43

CHAPTER 1

My Dad

Today was Father-Daughter Day. My Dad took me to the Brookfield Zoo. We walked from cage, to enclosure, to aviary. We peered through every glass aquarium and terrarium. My father loved animals. And I loved them, too. My Dad always stopped at the polar bears. He pulled out a big bag of fluffy white marshmallows, his special treat for his "favorite" polar bears. One by one, he tossed marshmallows to the polar bears. He took careful aim, making sure the bears could catch the marshmallows easily; in their mouths, or with their paws. My Dad was a hero! Visitors can no longer feed zoo animals, nowadays. Evil ones threw harmful objects into animal enclosures. Or, poisoned them.

I was a lucky child. My parents were happily married. My father's goal was to provide a beautiful home for his wife and children. He took me along as he did home repairs. "Hand me the hammer." "The wrench." "The screwdriver." He taught me the names of his tools. He explained what he was doing, step by step. And why he was doing it. He invited me into his workshop. My Dad built storage cabinets and furniture for our home. He "built-in" our bedrooms; crafting beds, dressers, and desks. Both parents worked to make our home beautiful, indoors and out. By age 10, I, too was laying floor tile, and planting trees. Woodworking was my father's hobby. He earned his income as an engineer. He allowed me into his office, and taught me how to use a compass and a slide-rule. Father-Daughter Day on the job, he brought me along to the lab.

Just as my mother pinched pennies at the grocery store to buy magazines, both parents pinched pennies to buy books for us kids. My

Dad built a bookshelf over my bed. It housed my collection of "Little Golden Books". Every night, My Dad "tucked me into bed". He read a "Little Golden Book" bedtime story. My Dad worked 8 hours every day. He attended college classes most evenings. If time allowed, he listened patiently, as I read the bedtime story back to him. When I grew older, I read bedtime stories to my little brother. And one day, I read bedtime stories to children of my own.

America's children attend school to learn. Reading, writing, and arithmetic. Once students learn the basics, teachers assign compositions. Creative writing encourages students to think for themselves. "What I did During Summer Vacation" is a popular topic, upon returning to school in the fall. "My Hero" is another favorite. Students are instructed to choose an historical figure, an athlete, or a celebrity. Many choose "My Dad".

"My Dad is a hero because he saves lives." Dads have exciting careers as police officers, firefighters, and doctors. Their children beam with pride. Others make contributions to their communities. They are coaches and youth-leaders. Some children tell stories of adventures with Dad. The camping trip, fishing on Saturday mornings, or a visit to an amusement park. Some report Dad is their hero because he does everyday things. "He takes care of my mom and me." These children are happy because, "My Dad pays attention to me". Farm dads take children along to feed animals, mend fences, plow fields, and harvest crops. City dads take children with them to walk the dog, run errands, and take out the trash. Attentive dads work on hobbies with their children, and play boardgames. Attentive dads take their children hiking and swimming. They participate in sports. They help with homework. And they watch movies together as a family. "My Dad is always there for me, when I need someone to talk to." A reliable, trustworthy Dad is a hero!

Ideally, couples marry "young and in love". They are devoted to each other's happiness and best interests. They unite to build a strong, secure marriage team. As a team, they work hard every day to build a safe, beautiful home in which to bring forth children. Together, as a team, they raise their children. They pay close attention to each child's nutrition, health, and education. Each child learns the difference between right and wrong. Each child learns to respect himself and others. Each child grows up to be a happy, healthy, productive adult. The perfect marriage provides a perfect home. Perfect parents raise perfect children, who enjoy a perfect childhood. Our hope is to live in a perfect world. Do you live in a perfect world?

Most of us live in the real world. We must "play the hand of cards we are dealt". This real world needs heroes. Heroes "step up to the plate". Heroes try their hardest to be the best they can be, and do the best they can do, each and every day. Most men have the ability to become biological fathers. This is the easy part. Parenting takes time, hard work, money, and love. Dads are devoted to their children. It takes a Real Hero to become a Real Dad.

Do you know where your children are? Find your children. Sadly, some parents are divorced. Other parents never married. Unfortunate children are orphans. Some of these orphans lost fathers before they were born. Parents and children can be adoptive, foster, or step. If you are a father, with children "out there, somewhere", find your children. Your goal is to become the Dad you always wanted for yourself. Do you need to "turn your life around"? Do you need to make amends? Turn your life around. Make amends. You are a hero! Heroes are "Dads".

Every family is unique. Are you a good husband and father, living "at home" with your family? Upgrade your skills. Participate in marriage encounters, family retreats, and parenting classes offered by your church, or in your community. Read "Parents" magazine. Set aside a regular "Family Day" each month. Set aside a "Father-Daughter Day" and a "Father-Son Day" each month. How many children do you have? Every child deserves Dad's undivided attention, and his own special "Day". You and your wife deserve "Date Night", and an occasional "Honeymoon Vacation". You both need your partner's undivided attention, free from the cares of the real world.

Was "My Dad" your childhood hero? Celebrate your Dad. America celebrates "Father's Day". Do something special for him. Can you call, or visit? Can you spend time alone with him, giving him your undivided attention? Can you ask him for advice? Are grandparents an active part of your children's lives? Unite your family. The more family members your child has in his life to love and guide him, the richer your child's childhood will be. Be a hero to your family. Be a hero to "Your Dad".

Do you and your child's mother live apart? Are you the custodial parent? Do you, and your child's mother, share joint custody? Are you required, by the court, to pay child-support? Keep child-support payments current. Your child eats every day. If payments are in arrears, return to the court for the relief you need. Take on a second job to catch up child-support payments. Visitation is not predicated upon the payment of child-support.

When Dad is the custodial parent, it is possible that the mother is ordered to pay child-support. Dad raises his children in his home, full-time. Mom gets visitation. Occasionally, mothers abandon their children. I know a single father whose wife abandoned the family to pursue alcohol and drugs. Her behavior changed. The children were no longer safe in her care. On visitation days, this father took his children to an "eat-in" pizza restaurant to visit Mom. He bought pizza and cold drinks for the table, then stood back at a reasonable distance, to supervise the goings-on. As the alcohol and drugs dug in, Mom missed more and more visits. Finally, she lost interest, altogether. She broke her children's hearts.

If you and your child's mother share joint custody, or if your child's mother is the custodial parent, leaving you with visitation rights, get your schedule "set in stone" by your local Family Court. This applies when the father has custody, and the mother has visitation rights, as well. Estranged parents often harbor animosity. Drama traumatizes children. Request neutral pick-up and drop-off locations. When school-agers go home for the weekend, with the non-custodial parent; picking the child up at school Friday afternoon, and dropping him off at school on Monday morning, works well. Clear alternate "chauffeurs" with courts and schools. If parental relations are toxic, minimize communications. Speak through the court. Hopefully, someday both parents will "grow-up".

Daycare and school placements require the approval of both parents and the court. Estranged mothers and fathers often have "new partners". Are your children safe in their care? Grandparents, Aunts, Uncles, and cousins need time with your children. Use common sense. Never leave your child, or children, with someone you can't trust 100%. Do ask the court to investigate every adult living in your child's, or children's custodial, or visiting home. The court will order a routine "welfare check".

The USA is a mobile society. Parents can live thousands of miles apart. In these cases, it makes sense for children to live with one parent during the school year, and the other parent during "spring break" and "summer vacation". You are no longer driving across town to pick up your child for the weekend. You must pay for expensive airline tickets, or road trips. Request the court "set" your custody and visitation schedule "in stone". And ask if there is help available to pay for transportation costs. NEVER ABANDON YOUR CHILD OR CHILDREN! This heartbreak is a wound that never heals. When money is "tight", communicate by phone. Send cards, letters, and gifts by mail.

Did you abandon your child, or children? Have you "turned your life around" 180 degrees? Are you ready to make amends? Do you need to "find" your children? Better now than never. Home DNA kits end "Baby Mama Drama", and solve the "mystery" of the "one night stand". Once you find a child who could be yours, professional lab tests are available. Don't expect teenagers, or young adults, to be "overjoyed" to meet you. Typically, they resent your absence. They will ask, "Why weren't you here for me?" Respond with willingness to "be here" from now, on. Forever. Be a hero! Be a Dad.

What happens when you encounter a "Baby Mama" you haven't seen for a long time? Have you both grown and matured? Are you both "still single"? Is it possible to begin a new relationship that leads to marriage? Or, a new relationship, in which both parents work together toward the best interests of your child? Approach the Family Court to decide matters of custody, visitation, and child-support. Heroes "do the right thing". Even if it means they need to pay child-support.

Prepare your home for your children. Ideally, the custodial parent needs 3 bedrooms. One for himself, one for girls, and another for boys. If you have only one child, or multiple same-sex children, then two bedrooms are fine. Make sleeping arrangements for "weekend visitors". This can be done in a three-room apartment by building a bunk into an alcove, (with your landlord's permission), or dividing a room with a decorative screen. A sofa bed works for "weekenders", as well as for overnight guests. If you "rent a room" from family members, is there a guest room in this home? A home was featured on HGTV where the retired couple added a "bunk room" for visiting grandchildren. Perhaps a "bunk room", in a two-bedroom home, would work for your "weekend warrior" children. Every child needs his own bed, and space to store his belongings. Your home becomes your child's home, too. Perhaps your child's dog, cat, or hamster will live in your home with you, full-time.

You may find your child living in a foster home, or with relatives other than his mother. Go to Family Court to obtain visitation. Learn your rights and obligations. Exercise your rights. Fulfill your obligations. Will you become your child's custodial parent? Is your child happy, safe, and secure at "home" with grandparents, or other relatives? Work with Family Court in the best interest of your child. You will be a hero! You will be a Dad. What if you discover that your child lives at a "youth ranch", or in a group home for children with "special needs"? Your child is where he needs to be. Work with Family Court and the facility, to meet your child's needs. Your child needs you to be an important part of his life. Be a hero! Be a Dad. If you learn that your child has been placed for adoption, add your name to the registry that reunites biological parents and children.

There are LGBTQ couples who wish to become parents. These couples can apply to foster, or adopt. Many LGBTQ individuals became biological parents, before "coming out". Your children love you. Your children need you. Be a hero! Be a Dad. Be a second Dad. Be a Mom. Be a second Mom. Regardless of the circumstance, be a hero!

I once heard a "happy ending" story. A single mother struggled to overcome adversity. Her two little children finally attended school, "all day". She now worked at her "dream job", earning good pay and benefits. Her new boyfriend promised to be "the love of her life". Until she told him, "We're pregnant". He packed his bags and moved away, never to be seen or heard, again. What could she do? Her friends stood beside her and offered support. Among them, a gay couple were hoping to adopt. Both enjoyed careers as professionals, and they lived in a beautiful home. The masculine partner accompanied her to pre-natal appointments, and served as her labor-coach. When Baby was born, this man signed his name as "father" on Baby's birth certificate. When Mother and Baby were discharged from the hospital, a happy Daddy took his baby home.

Men without children can be heroes! Mentor your little brothers and sisters. Take them "under wing". Be the "favorite uncle" to nieces and nephews. Be the "male role model" to fatherless children in your family. Be their "Dad". If you are the Godfather to a child, whether he has two parents, or not, take an active role in your God-child's life. Sign up to mentor youth in your community. Join Big Brothers-Big Sisters-Big Pride. Be a hero! Be a Dad.

CHAPTER 2

Our Father

Heroes are powerful. Power comes from God. Heroes wake up to an "Hour of Power" every morning. Your "Hour of Power" is your time spent with God, in prayer. If this "Hour of Power" is new to you, begin with the world's most well-known, and popular prayer. The "Our Father", otherwise known as "The Lord's Prayer".

"Our Father, who art in heaven, hallowed be thy Name.
Thy kingdom come.
Thy will be done, on earth as it is in heaven.
Give us this day our daily bread.
And forgive us our trespasses, as we forgive those who trespass against us.
And lead us not into temptation, but deliver us from evil."
Amen

After you pray this prayer, go back to the beginning. Meditate on every word, phrase, and verse. Ask, what does this prayer really mean? What are you telling God? Is God saying something to you?

"Our Father". We address Almighty God, the creator of the universe, the creator of all that exists, and of existence, itself, as "Our Father". This implies an intimate relationship with Him. God loves us. And we love God. Think deeper. At that very moment, when we, along with our partner, conceive a new human life, we become co-creators with God. Do we act as co-creators with God in other ways?

Be a Hero!

Life begets life. Do other living creatures act as co-creators, too? God loves all His creation. Loving God means loving His creation. How do we treat those we love? How do we hope our loved ones will be treated by others? You love your wife. You love your child. You love your mother. Do you hope for them to "get along", and treat each other well? Do you love your neighbor? Does God?

Take all the time you need to meditate upon this prayer.

Do you know the Bible story of The Ten Commandments? God, Himself, wrote these Ten Commandments on two stone tablets. He gave these tablets to Moses, to present to His people. These Ten Commandments are an awesome gift. "Thy kingdom come." When everyone conducts himself according to The Ten Commandments, we live in safety, free from attack. There is peace and prosperity for all. Our world is a better place.

The Ten Commandments

1. I am the Lord your God. You shall not have strange gods before me.
2. You shall not take the Name of the Lord, your God, in vain.
3. Remember to keep holy the Sabbath Day.
4. Honor your father and your mother.
5. You shall not kill.
6. You shall not commit adultery.
7. You shall not steal.
8. You shall not bear false witness against your neighbor.
9. You shall not covet your neighbor's wife.
10. You shall not covet your neighbor's goods.

The Ten Commandments are found in the New American Bible: Exodus Chapter 20, verses 1-18.

Meditate upon each of The Ten Commandments during your "Hour of Power". Ask, what do each of these Commandments encompass? What does each Commandment mean? How does each Commandment apply to my daily life? Heroes obey The Ten Commandments.

make our world a better place. Heroes practice The Golden

o others as you would have them do unto you." The Golden Rule is found in the New American Bible: Matthew Chapter 7, verse 12 and Luke Chapter 6, verse 31.

Meditate upon The Golden Rule, during your "Hour of Power" Imagine yourself in the other person's place. How do you wish to be treated? Imagine yourself in an animal's place. How do you wish to be treated? God loves His whole creation. When you give your child a gift, do you hope he will treasure it? Do you expect him to destroy your gift, or treat it well? God is our Father. Creation is His gift to us, His children. "Hallowed be thy Name." Heroes honor God. Heroes treat all God's creation, well.

Keep copies of The Lord's Prayer, The Ten Commandments, and The Golden Rule close at hand. Look them up online, and print copies for yourself. Tape these copies to the back of your bedroom door, so you can read them every day. Or, buy beautiful posters to frame. Hang these posters on a wall inside your home. Everyone needs "a code to live by". Heroes choose The Lord's Prayer, The Ten Commandments, and The Golden Rule.

Begin writing a journal during your "Hour of Power". You will need a notebook and a pen. Write your journal as if you are writing a letter to God. Date each page. Your journal will become your examination of conscience. Write about your problems and anxieties. Write about decisions you struggle to make. Write about events. Write about interactions with others. Write your true emotions. Write your dreams and goals. Write whatever comes to mind, today. This is your journal.

At regular intervals, read your collection of journal entries. Read them as if your friend wrote these letters to you. Ask, how can I help my friend? Ask, how can my friend help himself? Often, solutions to problems "jump off the page". Realizations "jump off the page", as well. Is there "something" about myself that I need to change? Could I have responded to a circumstance, differently? Your journal "opens the door to your spirit". Your journal offers "insight". Acting upon "insight" opens the door to a better life, for yourself and others around you. You are becoming a hero!

There is a very important page to include in your journal. It's called a "Gratitude List". Number from one to ten. List ten things you are thankful for. If time is short, look around you. Number from one to three. List three things you are most thankful for, today. An "attitude of gratitude" teaches us to place our problems and anxieties into perspective. An "attitude of gratitude" is a positive attitude. A positive attitude is the best way to start your day. Take your positive attitude with you, wherever you go. "Attitudes" are "contagious". Your positive attitude uplifts everyone you encounter, along your way. Your positive attitude is powerful. Heroes are powerful. Be a hero!

Heroes read and learn. What better way to learn how to be a hero, than to read about heroes who have gone before? The Bible is the inspired Word of God. The Christian Bible is a library of 66 to 72 books. There are many translations. Choose the translation that is right for you. There is Hebrew Scripture, and a Muslim Koran. Read your Bible during your "Hour of Power", or at bedtime.

Heroes are "up to the challenge". You can read your entire Christian Bible in 66 to 72 months, one book each month, like a "book-of-the-month club". There are guidebooks to help you read your entire Bible in one year. There are Bible studies, like "The Bible Timeline", that "speed-read" you through. Or, you can "set your own pace" by reading one chapter, or one story each day. Meditate upon what you just read. Join a Bible study at your church. If your church doesn't offer a Bible study, start one of your own. Do you listen to Christian radio? Many stations offer Bible study, online.

Heroes are spiritual leaders. Heroes attend church every Sabbath. And every Holy day. Exercise your "freedom of religion". Attend the church, synagogue, mosque, or temple of your choice. Faith communities work together to help others, and uplift their communities, as a whole. Faith communities feed the hungry, shelter the homeless, and "turn lives around". They build hospitals and care facilities. They educate children and adults by building schools. They operate daycare centers.

By working together with your church community, you can accomplish more than one person working alone. If you don't already belong to a church community, join a "mainstream" church, now.

As a spiritual leader, you will take your wife and children to church with you. If you are unmarried, take your girlfriend. Take your sisters and brothers, nieces and nephews, and cousins. Pick up elderly parents and grandparents. Or, elderly aunts and uncles. Drive them to church. Arrange to meet adult friends and family members, there. If you participate in the Big Brothers-Big Sisters-Big Pride program, take your "Little" to church with you. As a Godfather, you are responsible for your God-child's religious training. Does he attend church with his parents? Take your God-child to church with you. Invite elderly, or disabled, neighbors to accompany you to church. You are a hero!

Imagine, for one moment, that God is a Super-hero. God is the source of power. God is in control. Do heroes ever feel weak? God is the source of strength. Do heroes ever feel afraid? God is the source of courage. When you need more power, more strength, and more courage to meet life's challenges, call on your Holy Father. Pray. He knows what you need. He knows what is best for you. He knows what the future holds. Trust God. Miracles happen every day!

CHAPTER 3

My Hero

Good husbands are heroes. Traditionally, the husband's role is to provide for, and protect his wife and children. He supplies the manpower. The wife's role is to be the nurturer and homemaker. Her body is designed to produce offspring and nourish them. Human offspring require attention 24 hours per day, 7 days per week, until they reach the age of reason. They require "hands on" care. This is the mother's job. They require ongoing education and guidance into adulthood. Both parents are needed to participate. These roles are assigned by DNA.

Both husbands, and wives, can work at their respective careers in the marketplace. Both can share domestic responsibilities. Once the children come along, everything changes. Marriage is designed to unite a couple for the purpose of building a home, and raising a family. Parents work together to raise their children to become happy, healthy, productive adults. Our children hold the future in their hands.

Marriage is a vocation. A vocation requires a lifetime of devotion. Your vocation is your "purpose", your reason to live. It is like a career and a "family business" rolled into one. Vocation means "called by God". God is Love. Love calls the husband and wife to unite as a team. Imagine your coach sketching your team's next play. Your coach has a plan. Each team member is assigned a job. When each player does his job, well; your team wins.

Sketch your "Team Marriage" game plan. Draw an equilateral triangle. Draw your triangle with its base, formed by two angles, at the bottom. Draw the third angle at the top. Sketch a team member at each angle, or "point". The position at the top is God. The husband and wife each take their positions at an angle that forms the base. God reaches down. The husband and wife each reach up. They hold hands with God. Then the husband and wife reach across the base to hold hands with each other. God is the captain of your team, and your "marriage coach". By holding hands, you have formed a "sacred circle". It is impenetrable. Place your children in the center of the circle. Draw a line from each angle to your children in the center. They are protected. God, the father, and the mother will "carry them in arms of love". Move forward together, as a strong and mighty team. Your goal is to win life's "Super Bowl".

What happens when a player doesn't show up on game day? There is no one to "throw a pass", or "catch the ball". How can this team win the game? This is what happens to single-parent families. Or, families in which there is a dysfunctional partner, who doesn't do his, or her, job. The absent partner leaves his position empty. The dysfunctional partner takes up space in the home, eats food, and causes chaos. He becomes a burden to those around him. He doesn't do his job. He "lets his team down". Nobody wins.

The "responsible partner" is left to carry the team. He now plays two positions. Can he do two full-time jobs? Can he be in two places at once? Is he "thrown into" a defensive position? How long can he hold off the opposition? We need strong marriage teams to build strong families. Strong families build strong communities. Strong communities build strong states. Strong states build strong nations. Build a strong family. Be a hero!

Everyone is called to his own special purpose. Everyone is not called to the vocation of marriage. Everyone is not called to be a parent, or raise a family. Be honest with yourself. Be honest with God. Be honest with your "intended". Talk about your expectations, before you marry. Write, sign, and notarize a prenuptial agreement contract. This is common sense. 50% of marriages end in divorce.

Marriage promises to be fun! Men and women, both need attention, recognition, and appreciation. We all crave love and affection. Adults need sex. The husband and wife live together in the same home. Through good times, and bad, they are there for each other. Marriage is not a 50-50 proposition. Marriage requires each partner to give 100%.

Sex is the glue that holds your marriage together. Sexual relations form strong and powerful bonds. And sex is fun! The monogamy of marriage, along with proximity, promises healthy sex in abundance. It is said that "sex is God's wedding present to the bride and groom". During Bible times, and until relatively recently, teenagers married shortly after the onset of puberty. This practice made virginity until marriage, possible. Today's Western Culture delays marriage in favor of a lengthy education. In order to guarantee the continuation of our species, DNA programs a strong and powerful sexual desire within us. Today, many of us "open the present, early".

Marriage partners are friends. You have a "built-in" escort to events. And a date for Valentine's Day. You go on vacations and outings together. You enjoy fireside chats. Marriage partners are business partners, building the family home, and family fortune. Marriage partners are parenting partners. Although parenting is hard work, raising a family is rewarding. And children are fun!

Children take delight in the smallest adventures. A walk to the park, playing on the playground, followed by a trip to the ice cream store is a special day. Children love swimming, sledding, and learning to ride their bikes. We watch our children grow, and marvel at their accomplishments. Our babies learn to walk, then run. Soon they play on sports teams. Our babies learn to talk, then read. Soon they graduate high school, diploma in hand. We will always remember baking cookies together, on a "snow day". Nothing beats Thanksgiving and Christmas with the family. We treasure these moments, forever.

Always be where you are supposed to be, doing what you are supposed to do. "Cheating" on your partner is adultery. Marriage is built on love. How do we treat those we love? How do you wish to be treated by your loved one? Marriage is built on trust. Betrayal of trust hurts the one who is betrayed. Betrayal breaks hearts. It causes deep wounds that, once healed, leave scars. Marriage is built on mutual respect. What happens if the cheater brings home a disease? What if an affair ends in pregnancy?

Adultery harms your children. Your happy, secure, and stable marriage keeps them safe. Strong marriages build strong families. Strong families build strong communities. Strong communities build strong nations. Build a strong marriage. Be a hero!

Infidelity is not the only way to cheat on your spouse. I once helped a newly divorced friend move. She rented a home for herself, and the one, of two children, she kept to raise. The older child lived with Daddy. She had sold the marital home. Her ex-husband took out a large equity loan on the property, without her knowledge or consent, before running off with his new girlfriend. "You shall not steal." Both partners worked hard to buy and pay for that home. She got nothing in return. A few months later, Daddy returned his teenage daughter to Mama. Why? She was pregnant.

A TV court show brought a "super cheater" to light. He defrauded two ex-wives. Ex number 2 was suing him. She just sold the marital home she had been awarded in their divorce decree. Following their divorce, this woman worked hard to pay off the house. Then she sold it. She received $125.00 from this sale. Ex number 1 (or the state, on her behalf), had put a lien on the property for child-support. This "deadbeat dad" owed 18 years-worth. It gets "better". Wife number 3 stood by him in court. He had become a "house-husband". He "baby-sat" her school-age son (who attended school all day) as she worked to support him.

Women can be as deceitful as men. They marry for money. Honeymoon over, they file for divorce. They walk away with half of everything he worked hard for. There are many good arguments in favor of the prenuptial agreement contract. No matter how much you love each other on your wedding day, sometimes, "even good apples go bad".

Get a job! Get two jobs, if needed. Go back to school to upgrade your skills, and earn more money. Start a business of your own. Real men work hard every day. Respect yourself, and others. Men are, by nature, competitive. Compete to own the best home, and provide the highest income, to support your wife and children. Compete to be the "Husband and Father of the Year".

Get a hobby. Go fishing. Go hunting. Plant a vegetable garden. Feed your family. Try your hand at woodworking, restore vehicles, pursue a music career, part-time. Lock yourself in your office to write. Perhaps you will earn extra money. Participate in sports, work-out, take martial arts classes. Buy a gun and learn to use it. Learn to care for it. Practice gun safety, and target shooting at the range. Protect your home and family. Take classes offered at the library, or DIY store. Learn the basics of home maintenance and repair. A real man is "Mr. Fix It". The leaky faucet and stopped up drain are "your job". Do your job. Real men are heroes.

Does your wife "nag" you? Do you "sit around the house in your underwear", indulging in "bad habits"? Real men wake up, shower, dress in clean clothes, roll up their sleeves, and get to work. Even on "days off". If you and your wife are exhausted, and treating yourselves to "a day off in bed", shower and dress in clean pajama bottoms. Real men assume adult responsibility. Be a hero! Clean up your own mess.

Mothers and homemakers are expected to work hard all day at home, as husbands work hard all day in the marketplace. She is expected to raise your children. She is expected to clean house and do laundry. She is expected to prepare home cooked meals "from scratch", and bake. She, too, has productive hobbies. She can make craft items to sell. Or, babysit to earn extra money. She can decorate your home. She can refinish furniture, and paint ceilings and walls. She can sew, quilt, garden, mow grass, and shovel snow. She shops, runs errands, and chauffeurs children to activities. If you have pets, she is expected to care for them. Homemaking improves everyone's quality of life. Homemaking is an important vocation. Homemakers are "worth their weight in gold".

Is your wife still dressed in her housecoat when you get home from work? Is your home in disarray? Did she spend her day scrolling through social media? Or watching TV? If she doesn't want to work as a homemaker, insist she get a job! Her earnings will pay for daycare. Real women wake up, shower, dress in clean clothes, roll up their sleeves, and get to work. Homemaking is a necessity. When households lack a full-time homemaker, husband, wife, and school-age children share the workload. Both marriage partners are trusted to be where they are supposed to be, doing what they are supposed to do. Even when you are apart, you are working toward the same goal. You are building a strong marriage team.

Yes, real men can be "house-husbands". "Full-time Dad and homemaker" is the accurate, and respectful title. Not many, but a small percentage of men are "called" to this vocation. This Dad can't wait to get up in the morning and tend to his family's needs. He looks forward to making vegetable soup, and baking a pie. He keeps his home clean and well-organized. His plan for today (unless something happens to change it) is to work in the garden. We are all individuals with hopes and dreams. Who expects his daughter to grow up to be a coal miner? A plumber, or an electrician? There are very few "male" or "female" professions, today. Your daughter can become the Governor of your state! Just as you are proud of your successful daughter, be proud of your successful son. The full-time Dad and homemaker. He is a hero!

Marriage is a team effort. Both partners work together. As children grow, they take their places in the family "workforce". No one is "spoiled". No one is "too good to work", or do his "fair share". The "house-husband", lounging at home in his underwear, is as useless as the "house-wife", lounging in her housecoat, all day. These dysfunctional "partners" take up space in the home, eat food, and eventually cause chaos. No one can depend on them. They become "burdens" to their families. Employers fire non-productive workers. Exasperated partners "kick them to the curb". Don't be a "lazy bum". Be a real man. Be a hero!

Marriage retreats are designed to build strong marriage teams. Church-based couples' groups are designed to help make good marriages, better. Parenting classes offer good parents helpful advice and support. Participate in these groups. When problems arise, seek pastoral counseling. Provide for, and protect your wife and children. Supply the manpower. Good husbands are heroes. Be a hero!

Every hero is not called to be a husband and father. There are many vocations. And many heroes are not ready to become husbands and fathers, now. Do not place yourself in a position where you must make difficult choices. Be a hero by practicing safe sex. Always use a condom.

Love calls the husband and wife to unite in marriage. Love calls them to bring forth children. Put love first in your marriage, every day. Wrap your arms around your wife. Hold her, kiss her, love her. Provide for her and protect her. Tell her everything will be okay. Heroes are loving, gentle, and kind. Your wife is safe and secure. She can focus her attention on your children. She can wrap her arms around them, hold them, and nourish them in every way. Mothers are loving, gentle, and kind. Wrap your arms around your family. Love your family. Keep your home and family safe and secure. Husbands and fathers are heroes!

CHAPTER 4

Soar With Eagles

Real men, and real women, love our country. Real men, and real women, love the USA. We are patriots. Patriots are heroes. Heroes are strong warriors, who serve in our nation's armed forces. They fight for our country. They defend our US Constitution, and keep every American, safe. Be a hero. Sign up to serve in our military. Enlist in the Army, Navy, Airforce, Marines, or Coast Guard. Enlist in the home-based National Guard. Your enlistment can lead to a military career. Or, following your tour of active duty, you can remain in the Reserves. Reserve duty is a part-time job that requires you to work one weekend a month, and two weeks per year. You receive good pay and benefits. If you are a US Citizen, or resident alien, between the ages of 17-34, who has not yet served in our military; see your recruiter, today.

Basic military training serves as a "finishing school" for young adults. This is where we learn to, "Be all you can be". And this is where we learn "it's not all about me". Basic training teaches teamwork. Teamwork saves lives. Basic training teaches respect for self and others. Basic training teaches adult responsibility. Basic training instills discipline. Basic training builds strength, courage, and confidence. Recruits graduate basic training as "functional adults". Graduates "can do". Basic training builds heroes.

Military service provides ongoing training and education. In addition to infantry soldiers, sailors, and airplane pilots; there are physicians, dentists, nurses, and a variety of healthcare personnel. There are attorneys, teachers, technicians, drivers, and clerks. There are barbers, mechanics, cooks, specialists, and more. Military service provides job experience that is valuable in the civilian workforce, once discharged. Benefits offered to veterans include "points" toward civil service jobs, and "preference" toward civilian jobs.

What military service lacks in paycheck dollars, it makes up in benefits. Single adults receive food, clothing, housing, and medical-dental care, free. Single adults can budget a small personal allowance from their paychecks, and bank the rest. They look forward to well-funded savings accounts, upon discharge. Married personnel plan "flexibility" into family life. If both parents are active duty, then children must have a guardian. Children need to be raised in a stable home. Active-duty personnel can be deployed at any time.

Military families are special. Usually, the husband is active duty, and the wife is not. Sometimes, it is the wife on active duty, instead. Military benefits extend to military family members, and the military spouse receives an "allotment check". Families are not housed in the barracks. Therefore, family members do not receive food, clothing, or housing. If this family is fortunate, there is housing available to rent on post, or base. Otherwise, they must provide their own. Military spouses often work, to make ends meet.

VA benefits include home loans. It is possible to purchase a home "outside the gates". The VA program allows you to purchase a 1-4 family home. It is wise to purchase a multi-family home. Your rental income helps make the payments. When you are called to move, it is easier to hire a rental management company to manage apartments. If 1 unit is vacant, you continue collecting rent from the occupied unit, or units. There will be money to pay your manager, mow grass, and make repairs. Proximity to a military installation guarantees your rentals will remain full.

Many family members and friends served in our military. They bought homes. As soon as they "got settled in", they received orders to move, again. It makes more sense to save a large portion of your paycheck each month, to purchase your home upon discharge, or retirement. Some military families buy homes in their "home towns". The wife, or husband, lives in the home with their children, close to family and life-long friends. The whole family is together when the active-duty husband, or wife, comes home on leave. Spouses with RV's can take the family to spend summers together at an RV park, inside, or outside, the gates. Moderate climates allow families to live in RV's year-round. "Bunkhouse" models offer separate sleeping quarters for parents, and children.

Military families learn to "travel light". They move from state-to-state, and overseas. Military life is an adventure. Single military personnel may wish to fill a public storage unit before "leaving home". Pre-pay, or auto-deduct payments from your checking account, or credit card, to avoid the hassle of paying bills each month. Your parents may wish to retire and move to Florida, once you are gone. They are unable to store your belongings. A friend generously offered to store my belongings in her basement, while I was "on the road". Her basement flooded. Everything got wet, and was thrown away.

The military becomes your "home and family". Many personnel go "home on leave" to visit family and friends. My daughter went "home on leave" with a "buddy" who lived in Queens. She enjoyed a tour of New York City, and made new friends.

VA benefits include education, shopping at the commissary and PX, and many, many others. Print out a list. Many businesses offer military discounts for active-duty personnel and veterans. Some discounts, like airline tickets, are not advertised. Always ask. It pays to be a hero. VA medical benefits are yours, for life. Make a list of benefits to which you are entitled, and use them.

Veterans serve veterans. And veterans serve their communities. Employers sponsor veterans' groups "on the job". Churches sponsor veterans' groups within their congregations. These veterans participate at community events, and assist at funerals. They raise funds for worthy causes. Veterans are heroes.

Everyone is not able to serve in our military. Be a hero! Serve our country at home. Run for public office. Campaign for worthy candidates, and important issues. VOTE! Help others in your community through volunteer work. Participate in church activities and charitable good works. Participate at your child's school. Coach a sports team. Lead a scouting troop. Serve on your local volunteer fire department. Serve on your neighborhood block watch. Donate time and money to your local animal shelter. Those who serve are heroes!

There is a saying, "birds of a feather, flock together". The phrase "soar with eagles" means, "associate with good, hardworking, successful people". Do you have time to waste, hanging out with drunks and drug-addicts? With gang-bangers, or criminals? With drama queens, or trouble-makers? In a word, NO!

What kinds of birds flock together in your neighborhood? Are you surrounded by gang-bangers, violent criminals, and thugs? Do you need to move? Turn to a blank sheet of paper in your journal. Draw a vertical line down the middle. Write STAY at the top left. And GO at the top right. List your reasons to stay, or go. Then decide. A valid reason to stay may be that you get "free", or low-cost, rent in Grandma's home. She needs companionship, and someone to "help out". She needs protection. As a widow, she is emotionally attached to the home that Grandpa bought for her, years ago. This home, once filled with children's laughter, is filled with memories, today.

Reasons to go include violence in the streets, frequent burglaries, and vandalism. Your car is unsafe parked on the street. Or, even locked in your garage! Your children cannot leave home unescorted. Or, even play in your fenced backyard! Schools are failing. Buildings are "falling down". And, the landscape is littered with trash.

If you stay, can you make a positive change? Do you have the time and energy needed to organize an effective neighborhood block watch group? Can you organize a "clean-up" campaign? Can you rally your local officials to make improvements, like adding street lights, and filling potholes? Can you organize neighbors to apply for "block grants" to improve housing units? Can you improve home security by building a concrete wall around your property? Can you install a home security system? Do you own a well-trained dog? Can you speak up at school board meetings? Or, take your seat as a school-board member? Heroes make a difference!

Do you need to move to a better neighborhood? Do your children need to attend better schools? Surprisingly, I once found an affordable apartment in an expensive Boston suburb, known for tranquility, and good public schools It was cheaper than a comparable apartment in the city, and located right across the street from the commuter train station. This apartment rented at a discounted price because it was located in a commercial building. It was on the second floor, above a popular restaurant. It didn't "fit-in" with the suburban, single-family home, lifestyle. Few people looked for apartments, here. Later, I owned a condo that featured an underground parking garage, along with shops and restaurants at street level. Located downtown, this condo represented luxury living. Many areas of our nation offer "school choice", and "voucher" programs, to pay for private schools. Investigate all your options. Decide what is right for you. Heroes make positive changes!

Heroes are where they are supposed to be, doing what they are supposed to do. Heroes can be found serving in our military. Heroes can be found at home, work, school, and church. Heroes work hard every day to build better lives. For themselves and their families, their communities, and the USA. On "days off" heroes enjoy outings with family and friends. They entertain family and friends at home. They spend "family time" with their wives and children. They work on hobbies, inviting family and friends to participate. Heroes soar with eagles!

CHAPTER 5

"Truth, Justice, and the American Way"

According to Wikipedia, Jerry Siegel and Joe Shuster created Superman for DC Comics in 1938. He was a super "man" from a distant planet, with super human powers. The following year, 1939, World War II broke out. With the bombing attack on Pearl Harbor in 1941, the USA was drawn into the fray. "Truth, Justice, and the American Way" became Superman's motto, and America's call to arms.

Clark Kent was "human" like you, and me. He worked as an investigative journalist. When crime threatened law-abiding citizens, Clark Kent donned his "Superman" gear, and got to work. He rescued innocent victims from the clutches of criminals, caught in the act of harming them. In 1945, World War II ended. By 1952, "The Adventures of Superman" appeared on TV. This program lasted until 1958. And then, there were re-runs. Millions of American youth were enthralled. Boys, and girls, longed to possess super powers. Boys hoped to grow up to be Superman. Superman remains a "super star" to this day.

By the 1960's, these children were growing up. "Truth, Justice, and the American Way" filled our hearts and minds. We wanted to bring truth and justice to all Americans. And, make our world a better place. The "hippie" movement was on. We became "flower children", advocating love and peace. Our mission was "to right society's wrongs". Our mission was to bring truth and justice to the whole world.

By the 1960's, Jim Crow had held America hostage long enough. We joined the Civil Rights Movement, under the leadership of The Reverend Dr. Martin Luther King, Jr. Our goal was to right these wrongs. Between 1957 and 1991, our Congress passed Civil Rights legislation. The "landmark" Civil Rights Bill was signed into law by President Lyndon B. Johnson in 1964. Dr. King was a wise, and charismatic, leader. You can watch him, and hear him, online, as he delivers his "Dream" speech. MLK was a hero!

The Vietnam war lasted 20 years, from 1955 to 1975. Americans empathized with the freedom-loving people of South Vietnam. They wanted to work at their jobs, operate their businesses, and farm their lands. They wanted to educate their children, and worship according to the religion of their free choice; just like us. The South Vietnamese people hoped to live in peace.

Powerful Communist nations attacked them indirectly, led by China and the USSR. "Reunification" of Vietnam was their ploy. What did the Communist attackers want? Everything! Like most attackers, the Communists hoped to rob South Vietnam of everything its people owned. The USA came to South Vietnam's defense. These Communist attackers were America's enemies, too.

America's "flower children" demonstrated on our university campuses, in our streets, and at our National Mall in Washington, DC. We demanded an end to the Vietnam War. Our own government had become the problem. The "Cold War" between Communism and Western Civilization raged. All three "super powers" hoped to avoid a nuclear holocaust, at Vietnam's expense. Vietnam became the "chess board", on which they "played their war games". Instead of listening to military experts, who could end this war in a matter of weeks, politicians "played politics". These "politics" cost thousands of American lives. 58,220 American troops lie dead in the jungle. In 1970, at Kent State University, American blood spilled onto American soil. Finally, in 1973, American forces pulled out of Vietnam. Saigon fell to Communist dictatorship rule in 1975. Fortunate South Vietnamese are now American citizens.

Yes, those who fought, and those who died, in Vietnam are heroes. And those of us who demonstrated against a government that "played politics" with American lives, are heroes, too. Repercussions of the Vietnam War echo throughout America, today.

During 1964 and 1965. a plethora of government spending bills were passed by Congress. Among these bills were Medicare and Medicaid. LBJ sold America his "Great Society". It was LBJ's version of FDR's "New Deal". The entitlement programs enacted, are collectively known, today, as "Welfare". Welfare was intended to be America's "safety net". No one expected welfare to become a career choice. Taxpayers worked harder and harder, to pay higher and higher taxes. Single mothers gave birth to babies, to use as "meal tickets". With the exceptions of Medicare and Medicaid, the Great Society turned out to be a "Great Mistake".

Young American men, between the ages of 18-26, were required to register for "the draft". When his "number came up", the draft-card-holder was forced to join the US Army. He could avoid the draft by voluntarily enlisting in another branch of military service. All branches of the US military were eventually deployed to serve in Vietnam. Cowards ran away, and hid. Some ran as far as Canada. We called them "draft-dodgers". Some attended college, full-time; thus obtaining "deferments". Politicians obtained deferments for their sons. This angered taxpayers, who couldn't afford college for their own children. The military didn't accept criminals. And, recruits, unable to pass the "physical", were labeled 4F. Let's do the math.

The young men drafted into the Army, to fight the Vietnam War, were America's healthiest, brightest, and best. They were our future husbands and fathers. 58,220 troops were killed, leaving 58,220 American women without husbands. Who was left at home to father the next generation? Draft-dodgers, criminals, and 4F's are not husband material. College graduates, and military personnel who survived to return home, did not "provide enough husbands to go around". Single mothers gave birth. And taxpayers, struggling to support their own families, worked harder to support them. This divided Americans.

The percentage of single mothers, giving birth outside of wedlock, increases every year. Children raised in single-parent families are less likely to succeed. Children need two parents. Men, raised by single mothers, don't learn how to be husbands and fathers. Many don't even try. A high school girl was interviewed by an investigative journalist on TV. She said, "I can't wait until I have my baby, so I can get my apartment and my check". She wasn't even pregnant!

The "Great Mistake" creates poverty. Welfare income falls far below the poverty line. A homeless man was interviewed by an investigative journalist on TV. He was happy that our government gave him "free money". He collected $600.00 per month. No wonder he was homeless! Can you rent a home for $600.00 per month? Will $600.00 per month pay for all your basic necessities?

"You can't legislate morality." My high school history teacher frequently repeated this phrase. Along with her other "favorite", "Power corrupts, and absolute power corrupts, absolutely". What do these phrases mean to you? Let's do the math, again.

Her welfare check places the single mother, and her children, in poverty. Unless she lives with her parents, or other family members, who give her "free", or low-cost rent, she can't "make ends meet". She can't get a job, and work outside the home every day, without daycare for her children. Unless her parents, or other family members, "step up" to provide "free", or low-cost daycare, she is "stuck". Daycare is expensive. Most of the jobs available to single mothers don't pay enough to cover the high cost of daycare, along with other necessities. She depends on her "Baby Daddy" to supply the "extras", like formula and diapers. When the "Baby Daddy" fails, some women barter sexual favors. Reality is that few people will give her "something for nothing". Often, men are willing to "help out", as long as they "get something in return". Will this create another baby? Another "mouth to feed"? How many "favors" will she need?

Working divorcees depend on child-support payments to pay for daycare. "Deadbeat Dads", who fail to pay their child-support payments on time every month, force their ex-wives, and children, onto the Welfare rolls. "Deadbeat Dads" "fly under the radar". Once caught, they are forced to pay all that delinquent child-support. If the ex-wife collected Welfare, the amount she collected is paid back to the government, first. Any money left over goes to her, for her children.

"Good" men want to marry "good" women, and raise families of their own. Again, poverty rears its ugly head. Many hard-working men don't earn enough money to support a family. Their incomes only support bachelors. Today, young couples bypass the "alter", and simply "move-in together". They give birth. The "Baby Mama" applies for Welfare, as a single mother. Along with money, Welfare provides affordable healthcare benefits. This couple becomes a two-income family, able to "make ends meet". Is this fair to the hard-working taxpayers? Is this fair to the couple and their children? Wouldn't a Great Society provide affordable healthcare, and a low-cost public daycare system, instead of handing out Welfare checks? Affordable healthcare, and a low-cost public daycare system, allow more Americans to work, and pay taxes. They "level the playing field".

How do we "level the playing field" for our homeless population? The overwhelming majority of homeless Americans are disabled. They are alcoholics, addicts, and mentally ill. Many of them commit crimes. Wouldn't it make sense to lock them in supervised group homes, providing treatment and care? No, these people are not "free" to be homeless. They are unable to care for themselves. Let's pay taxes for social programs that work, instead of handing out "free money" to people who "don't". America's "Great Society" has become America's "Great Failure". Don't let it become America's "Downfall".

America's public servants must be held accountable. Our public servants must "do their jobs". Affordable healthcare, and low-cost public daycare, to support American families are possible. Eliminate "bureaus" that have outlived their usefulness. Eliminate government waste. Redirect public funds.

Americans know that strong marriages build strong families. Strong families build strong communities. And, strong families build wealth. Strong communities build wealth, as well. Strong and wealthy communities build strong and wealthy states. And ultimately, a strong and wealthy USA. What happens to America, when our families break down, one by one?

"Truth, Justice, and the American Way." When all Americans work together, toward the same goals, we become "Super Heroes", like Superman. The USA takes its rightful place on the "world stage" as a Super Power. Do your part. Be a hero!

CHAPTER 6

Heroes Save Lives

Heroes save lives. Start by saving your own. Do you wake up to an "Hour of Power" each morning? Have the Lord's Prayer, the Ten Commandments, and the Golden Rule become your "code to live by"? Do you start your day with an "attitude of gratitude"? Do you shower each morning, dress in clean clothes, roll up your sleeves, and get to work? Do one good thing to help yourself each day, and do one good thing to help others. Smile. Take your positive attitude with you, wherever you go.

None of us live in a perfect world. Every one of us has "problems". As we overcome our own problems, we help others. Heroes are alive. Heroes are healthy and strong. Heroes "can do". Heroes are courageous. And, heroes are smart. Heroes know that education, hard work, good conduct, and sound money management lead to success. Heroes read and learn. Are you reading your Bible? Add another book to your reading list. "Pull Yourself Up By Your Bootstraps" by Evelyn Cross.

Heroes are alive. Problems can kill. Killer problems are alcoholism, drug-addiction, untreated mental illness, and crime. We become heroes when we address these problems. Address these problems, now. Turn your life around! You will be a hero! By saving your own life, you save the lives of others.

Physical illness is a problem with killer potential. Become a builder. Build-up your body. Resolve your health issues. Build and improve your home. Whether you rent, or own, maintain your home in clean, well-organized, attractive condition. Maintain everything you own in clean, attractive, and functional condition. Build your career. Get a job. Upgrade your skills, and your paycheck, with education. Build a business of your own. Budget carefully. Build wealth. "Work hard, work smart, save, and invest." Help others along the way. Prepare to marry and raise a family. Build your community, your state, and your nation.

Time is a valuable resource. And, relationships are important. Heroes "soar with eagles". Until you are ready to marry, and raise a family; engage in positive, best-quality dating relationships with positive, best-quality partners. Engage in positive relationships with family, friends, co-workers, customers, and members of your church and community. Positive relationships are characterized by good manners and all due respect. Everyone's feelings are considered, and everyone's needs are addressed. Positive relationships are based on "enlightened self-interest".

Turn to a blank page in your journal. Write "Rules, Boundaries, and Limitations" at the top of the page. Write a list of rules, boundaries, and limitations for yourself, during your "Hour of Power". Examples are: "I will be gentle, loving, and kind." "I will respect myself and others." "I will not loan money." I will not loan my car, tools, or anything else I worked hard to pay for." "I will not tolerate negative behavior." Heroes are busy saving lives. Heroes have no time for negative behavior. When appropriate, heroes help others by giving time and money.

During your "Hour of Power", meditate upon "forgiveness". Forgiveness does not mean "tolerate". We give trespassers a second chance. Just as we need second chances, ourselves. We instruct and guide them, after pointing out the "error of their ways". We expect them to move forward, in a positive direction. Heroes do not tolerate ongoing negative behavior! First and foremost, heroes do not tolerate ongoing negative behavior in themselves. Heroes make positive changes. Heroes do not tolerate ongoing negative behavior in partners, family, friends, co-workers, customers, or members of their churches or communities. Heroes make positive changes. Even if the only positive change available, is to exclude negative people from your life. Is "hanging out" with "troublemakers" in your best interest? How many days of your life will you waste in a "toxic" relationship? Heroes "soar with eagles".

Heroes protect themselves and others. Heroes protect their own lives. Heroes protect their loved ones. Heroes protect their animals. Heroes protect their homes and property. Heroes protect innocent victims. Heroes stop violent attacks! Heroes "spring into action" when violence occurs. Heroes use every means necessary to stop the attack. If lethal force is the only means effective to stop the attack, the attacker made this choice. Attackers risk their own lives, by choosing to attack others. By stopping violent attack, heroes save lives!

Victims are victims. And, victims have rights. Attackers are criminals. And, criminals "surrender" their rights when they choose to attack. "We hold these truths to be self-evident, that all men are created equal, that they are endowed by their Creator with certain unalienable Rights, that among these are Life, Liberty, and the pursuit of Happiness." Do you remember these words from American history class? Thomas Jefferson, 1776, "The Declaration of Independence". When criminals attack, they deprive victims of their Civil Rights.

Today's "pop culture" is "soft on crime". It portrays criminals as "victims". "The Great Society", in other words, "The Great Mistake", created this. Mankind appeared on a planet equipped to meet all his needs. Mankind thrived because he was able to hunt and gather to feed himself. He was able to farm. Mankind was able to mine our planet's resources, and manufacture goods. Mankind was able to WORK to improve his life. Civilization was built upon mankind's WILLINGNESS TO WORK. The only humans ENTITLED to food, and benefits, without working to obtain them, are infants and young children. Animals, in our care, are entitled to food and benefits. Captivity prevents them from meeting these needs, on their own.

It was a "Great Mistake" to legislate that Americans are ENTITLED to food and benefits, even if they are UNWILLING TO WORK. Today, hard-working taxpayers are FORCED to share "the fruits of their labors" with those who REFUSE TO WORK. "You shall not covet your neighbor's goods." The word "covet" means "A SENSE OF ENTITLEMENT".

What kind of mother gives birth to a "meal ticket"? Is she concerned for her child's "best interests"? Or, is she "all about me"? Does she avoid working at a job, serving in our military, or studying in school? How does she contribute to her community? Or, to society as a whole? Yes, many good mothers are "forced" onto the Welfare rolls. They work hard to "break free". But many more are dysfunctional. They neglect and abuse their children. Fathers are dysfunctional, as well. They abandon their partners and children. Many of these children develop disabilities. And many grow up to become criminals. And yes, they are victims. Every child deserves two parents who love him, focus positive attention on him, and raise him in a secure, stable family home. The "Great Mistake" broke down the American family. And, produced generations of criminals.

A Great Society provides "emergency assistance". Bad things happen to all of us. There are storms in life. No society provides for generations of people supported by Welfare. This idea is financially unaffordable, and unsustainable, as numbers of Welfare recipients grow. Recipients lose confidence in their own abilities to provide for themselves, and their families. They "give up". They refuse to "try". Real men provide for, and protect, their wives and children. When our government assumes the "husband and father role", men are "emasculated". They become "sperm donors", and a source of "entertainment". What does an unemployed, impoverished population do to entertain itself? Both men, and women, become "promiscuous". Husbands, and wives, are no longer obligated to work together, or to please each other. They no longer "need" each other. Families break down. When families break down, communities break down. Eventually, our entire nation crumbles.

The majority of black Americans descended from African slaves. Welfare hit black families, hard. Heroes read and learn. Read and learn American history. Slaves were controlled by fear of being "sold down the river". Once sold, the slave would never see his wife, and children, again. Families were torn apart. Conscientious slave owners kept families together. But, they, too, faced "problems". Slaves were confiscated, and sold, to pay debts. Once freed, African American families were overjoyed by the knowledge that their families would remain intact, for generations to come.

Freed slaves worked as share-croppers. They worked on the railroads. They started businesses of their own. They moved to cities, to work at high-paying factory jobs. They devoted themselves to their children's educations. They "saved every penny" for college. The first generation born free dreamed of becoming doctors, lawyers, and teachers. Until "The Great Society", black Americans lived in traditional families. They delighted in their children. They built homes and communities. They worked hard to achieve "The American Dream". Many acquired great wealth. Why are so many black Americans living in single-parent families, on Welfare, today? How did black America lose its momentum?

A Google check of stats reveals that, during the Vietnam War years, black Americans made up 11% of America's population. 16.3% of draftees were black. And 23% of the combat troops serving in Vietnam were black. And there lie America's healthiest, brightest, and best. There lie America's potential husbands and fathers. Potential husbands and fathers of all races lie dead in the jungle. Were those men alive today, they would be grandfathers, and great-grandfathers. Wars followed wars, following Vietnam. Wars take America's healthiest, brightest, and best.

Americans of all ethnicities receive entitlements. 20% of our population receives at least one entitlement. Children of all ethnicities grow up in single-parent families, in poverty, on Welfare. Since the dawn of human civilization, the MARRIAGE LICENSE has been the LICENSE TO BEAR CHILDREN! This is practical, "common sense". They say, "You can't legislate morality." The "Great Society" was a "Great Mistake". America legislated IMMORALITY! Our children pay the price. More than 50 years later, America's "War on Poverty" still isn't won. Mass casualties lie in its wake. How can we fix this? Heroes save lives.

Start by being a DAD! Be the best Dad you can be. To your own children. And to others. Be a husband. Be the best husband you can be. Teach boys to grow up to become husbands and fathers. Teach girls to grow up to become wives and mothers. Teach "Family Living" in our churches, and in our schools. Include LGBTQ individuals and couples, with all due respect. Many of these Americans are parents. By raising our children in loving, secure, stable homes, we provide opportunities for them to grow to reach their full potential. They become happy, healthy, productive adults. They achieve "The American Dream". Strong families build strong communities. Strong communities build strong states. Strong states build a strong nation. You can save the USA! Good husbands and fathers are heroes. Heroes save lives!

Become politically responsible. Advocate in favor of low-cost healthcare, and low-cost daycare, to replace Welfare. These items "level the playing field". Now, all parents are able to work, support their families, and pay taxes. Promote the "adoption option" for those unwilling, or unable, to raise children. Answer the prayers of childless couples, on their knees. Utilize America's public schools for their intended purpose. EDUCATE AMERICA'S CHILDREN!

For the record: Social Security Retirement Income is NOT Welfare. Social Security Retirement Income pre-dates "The Great Society". It began in 1935 as part of President FDR's "New Deal". Social Security checks are issued from a "retirement savings account". Workers deposit money into this savings account each, and every, payday. We deposit this money by way of FICA tax. Federal Insurance Contributions Act. Like other retirement savings accounts, this FICA account grows over time. After contributing the prescribed number of credits, and reaching the prescribed retirement age, taxpayers claim their Social Security benefits. Widows and widowers may claim either their spouses' benefits, or their own. This choice benefits life-long homemakers.

COVET: The FICA savings account grew and grew. Politicians "borrowed" money from this account, to pay for other programs. Today, retirees who worked all their lives, faithfully paying into FICA, are living in poverty. Heroes hold themselves accountable. Heroes hold others accountable. Do you hope to retire, someday? EVERY AMERICAN MUST HOLD OUR GOVERNMENT ACCOUNTABLE! All Americans are called to be heroes!

CHAPTER 7

Calling All Heroes!

NOW! Right now, today. We must fill our churches. Fill every church and chapel! Fill every synagogue! Fill every mosque! Fill every temple! Form lines through every holy door. Stretch them out for miles, around corners, and lengths of city blocks. SHOUT TO THE LORD! And PRAY!

God loves life. Every tiny life He created. Lives so tiny, our eyes can't see them, are of great value to God. God individually programmed every microscopic strand of DNA. He lovingly crafted our planet. Our universe. And, beyond. How valuable must we be? You, the individual, are very important to God. REPENT! Repent means "rethink". Turn your life around. Stand in the light of God's presence. STAND!

Your "inalienable rights" come from God. Communism, Socialism, Nazism, dictatorships, tyrannies, and evil isms of all sorts oppose God. Evil is on the attack. Evil covets. Evil governments announce they are entitled to attack, "for the greater good". This evil is not satisfied to steal your money, land, or material goods. This evil steals your inalienable rights. It steals your right to choose. Like slavery, it robs you of your opportunity to work, and attain good things for yourself. This evil covets your body, mind, and spirit. It covets your children, and your children's children. It robs you of your hope for the future. This evil causes suffering and pain. This evil causes destruction and death.

Awareness of God is programmed into our DNA. Humans instinctively "search" for Him. All the evil isms, dictatorships, and tyrannies oppose God. They demand to be worshipped, in His place.

And yes, evil tyrants invade churches. When congregations discover them, they walk away. God is "the Way, and the Truth, and the Life". New American Bible: John Chapter 14, verse 6. Jesus goes on to say, in verse 9, " ...Whoever has seen me has seen the Father". In John Chapter 10, verse 30, Jesus says, "The Father and I are one".

Faith-filled believers cannot be fooled. We will not worship a tyrant. When faith-filled believers, of all religions, fill houses of worship, we form a "hedge of protection" against evil attacks. God is our "refuge and our strength". New American Bible: Psalm 46, verse 1. God's people are FREE!

A Christian friend often laments that "denominations" are the work of the evil one, to keep God's children fighting among themselves. There are many "mainstream" religions around the world. We all worship the same God. Honor God by attending your house of worship. There is no need to argue. Or "talk the talk". Be a hero! "Walk the walk."

Are God's people "better" than everyone else? Or, does "goodness" lie in the fact that they "try"? We all make mistakes. Every morning brings a "new day", to begin our lives, anew. Wake up. Pray. Shower. Dress in clean clothes. Roll up your sleeves, and get to work. Do one good thing to help yourself. Then do one good thing to help others. Start at home, with yourself, and your family. Branch out into your community, your state, and your nation. What if every person obeyed The Ten Commandments, and practiced The Golden Rule? Would our world be a better place?

Heroes champion "Common Sense". Common sense tells us to hold ourselves accountable. Do you take good care of yourself and your family? Do you utilize your paycheck to first, pay your bills and provide necessities? Do you save money for "rainy days"? Or, do you spend uncontrollably, getting "caught short" when the rent is due, or you need to buy groceries? Do you do important jobs first, before leisure activities, or "play"? Do you hold your partner, children, and family members accountable? For example: children must complete "homework", or "chores", before going outdoors to play. Heroes must hold themselves, and others, accountable.

Heroes take an active role. We must build America's families. Our churches must act as "match-makers", bringing couples together. Teach marriage and family living in our churches, and in our schools. Strong families build strong communities. Teach girls to become wives and mothers. Teach boys to become husbands and fathers. Yes, both mothers and fathers work at careers. Teach families to work together, as teams. Support families with ongoing classes, activities, and counseling as needed. Strong families strengthen our communities. Strong communities build strong states. Strong states (and territories) build a strong USA. Hold our leaders accountable. Then the USA leads the world.

Our "success" comes from God. Good health and prosperity are the results of living according to The Ten Commandments and The Golden Rule. Have you noticed that church members appear to have "more" than everyone else in your neighborhood? They have an abundance of food, goods, and money to share with others. Why is that? Church members are "winners" because they "play for TEAM GOD". Play for the "winning team". Join a mainstream church, today. Play for TEAM GOD!

The single, most important, choice today's hero can make, is the choice to join a mainstream church. Become active in your church, and "stick close". Why? As a Dad, your role is to be the spiritual leader of your children. You teach them "right" from "wrong". As a husband and a father, your role is to be the "spiritual leader" of your family. As a "man", and a "hero", your role is to be a "spiritual leader" in your community. The Bible tells story, after story, of leaders. God takes "ordinary people", like you and me, and teaches them to become leaders. The Bible contains your leadership "instructions". It contains your "prosperity" instructions, as well.

The Bible teaches us the difference between "right" and "wrong". Heroes are leaders that hold themselves "accountable". We are accountable to God. Many people reject God, because they don't want to be held accountable. They want to do whatever they please, whenever they please, to whomever they please. They demand the reward that results from hard work, without working to achieve it. They watch and wait for opportunities to attack others. To steal what belongs to them. This is "criminal thinking". The criminal mind never reaches "the age of reason". It is "infantile" thinking. The criminal mind is focused on "me". Criminals don't care about the welfare of others. Criminals are "all about me".

By "sticking close" to our churches, we can depend on other church members to guide us, and encourage us. We are not "better" than anyone else. We just try our best, every day. We encourage ourselves, and each other, to "try harder". To walk the "straight and narrow path". We learn to be "on guard" against those who would discourage us. And most important, together we provide each other with "moral support".

Networking with church members helps us meet our needs. Networking with church members helps us meet the needs of others. Networking with church members helps us find jobs, housing, educational opportunities, dating partners, daycare, and wholesome activities for our children. Networking with church members helps us meet our needs for food, clothing, and household goods. Sometimes even lawn mowers, tractors, and cars! We help each other. As a Dad, you will take your children to church with you. As a husband and father, you will take your family to church with you. As a single man, you will go to church. Heroes participate in church!

Our children don't believe what we say. Our children believe what we do. Once disappointed, they never believe "empty promises", again. Every "bad" parent faces a "golden opportunity". The opportunity to repent, rethink, and turn his life around. You can become the Dad your children need. And you can become the Dad you always wanted for yourself. Turn your life around. We all make mistakes. Mistakes create obstacles that now, we must overcome. Encourage your children by overcoming your obstacles. They watch. They see. Your children learn that failure is a "normal" part of life. The "important part" of life is that we "get up and try again". We overcome. Take your children by the hand. They are "overcomers", too. Have you been a bad father? A bad husband? A bad citizen? A bad student? A bad employee? A bad neighbor? A bad son (or daughter)? Turn your life around! God will help you overcome.

There is a very special church, for very special people. This church is known for "working miracles". Its members call it "Big Church". Their "Bible" is called the "Big Book". Members love their church so much, they attend meetings there, every day. Sometimes even two, or three meetings in one day. This church is known as Alcoholics Anonymous. If you have a problem caused by alcohol, or drugs, let this be your church. The Twelve Steps are their Ten Commandments. The Golden Rule flows throughout their Big Book, based upon principles outlined in the Christian Bible. Members of this church help others, every day, as they help themselves.

Alcoholics Anonymous welcomes families. There are groups for wives, husbands, children and other family members, and friends. There is Al Anon, for the non-drinker, and non-user. There are groups for children. Addiction is a "family disease". Families need healing. And families need miracles! If you, or a family member, suffers from addiction, go to Alcoholics Anonymous-Al Anon, today!

America needs good men! More now, than ever before. America's families are in desperate need of good husbands and fathers. And every one of America's children needs a Dad. We need "tough guys", strong enough to protect us. We need men of courage. Not "punks" who rob our homes, or attack us on the streets. We need men of honor, who work hard to support their wives and children, Not "crybabies", begging for hot meals and warm beds. We need men who know what tools are for. Tools like the hammer, screwdriver, and saw. We need men who build things, and fix things. We need men who educate themselves and their children. We need Dads who discipline their children, and guide them toward profitable careers, that benefit society. Men who build themselves up to be the best they can be. We need men who do the best they can do, every day. AMERICA NEEDS HEROES!

America is dying of cancer. From the inside, out. Our children are failing. Without even trying, they "give up" and "drop out". Dreams are dying before our eyes. We don't need "social programs". We need women to be women. Where are the mothers, devoted to raising their children? Where are our homemakers? We need men to be men. Where are our workers? Our home-builders? Our community leaders? Are "daddies" scattered along our sidewalks, in ragged tents? Now is the moment. Now is the time. Every man in the USA must STAND UP! Dust yourself off. And GROW A PAIR! Be a man! AMERICA NEEDS HEROES!

CHAPTER 8

THINK!

Heroes think. Heroes think before they speak. And heroes think before they do. Heroes wake up to an "Hour of Power" every morning. During this Hour of Power, every morning, heroes THINK. God's birthday gift to each and every one of us is this: a body, mind, and spirit. God expects us to use these gifts, well. Use your mind to think.

Ask questions. Look up answers. Read and learn the facts. Reason using logic and math. Follow the money. "Connect the dots". Do you know the difference between good and evil? Right and wrong? Look up answers in your Bible, Scriptures, Koran, and Big Book. Pray.

Ask questions. Ask, "How will I make my life better, today?" Plan your day. Do one good thing to make your life better, today. Ask, "How will I make my child's life better, today?" Plan your day. Make your child's life better. Ask, "How will I make my partner's life better, today?" Plan your day. Make your partner's life better. Ask your way through your entire list of household members, including your dog. Ask your way through your list of family members. Ask your way through your list that includes job, business, school, church, and community. "Soar With Eagles." Ask, "How will I make America better, today?" As you work to improve your life, and the lives of those around you, you become a hero. You make our world a better place.

Ask, "Where does this Great Society lead?" What is the ultimate goal of the "welfare state"? Once the government pays all your bills, does the government become your boss? Do you become its slave?

How long does it take to check the weather and news, on your phone, every morning? Stay abreast of current events that may affect you. Read and learn facts. By learning one new fact, and applying what we have learned, we can improve our lives. By learning many facts, we can "connect the dots", and see the "whole picture".

Here is a fact: Do you know that our USA government breeds dogs to use as subjects of scientific experiments? I watched TV video shot at one of these kennels. These dogs are well fed, and well housed, using our taxpayers' money. They receive veterinary care. When humans approach, these dogs greet them enthusiastically. They wag their tails, and jump for joy. They willingly accompany these humans to the lab, where they are tortured in painful experiments. Is this how you want your hard-earned taxpayer dollars spent? Be a hero! Stop these experiments. Ask, "How can I make these innocent animals' lives better, today?"

When the "Great Society" was legislated, during the Vietnam War, medical science advanced at an exponential rate. Wounded veterans received "bionic" arms and legs. Modern technology led to "medical miracles". Today, Americans have joint replacement implants. We have heart pacemaker and defibrillator implants. Live donors bless loved ones, and even strangers, with kidney, and bone marrow, transplants. Americans are "walking around", alive today, thanks to pig valves implanted inside their hearts. Doctors are able to transplant hearts, lungs, kidneys, livers, pancreas, and other organs from "brain dead" donors. Almost every organ from the "newly expired" human can be harvested, and used to save many people's lives. We use eye, skin, bone tissue, and more.

Advances in modern medicine have created a market for transplantable organs. Where will these organs come from? Elderly patients, who die of "old age", cannot be organ donors. 70 year-old organs are "worn-out". Those who die from disease, leave diseased organs behind. We need young, healthy organs for transplant. These donors typically die from traffic accidents or gunshot wounds. Most of their organs are undamaged, and ready for transplant. THINK!

Why would our government pay to support an "underclass" of welfare recipients? Our government pays to feed them. Our government pays to house them in "projects"; or crime-ridden, inner-city neighborhoods, where they are at high risk of getting shot. And our government pays for their medical care. Just like the dogs in the kennels, bred to be subjects of cruel experiments, our government expects loyalty from these people. In the form of votes. Why doesn't our government "level the playing field" with affordable healthcare and daycare, instead? Then everyone can work his way out of poverty, and pay taxes.

American taxpayers pay huge amounts of money for education, but inner-city schools are failing. Teenagers "drop out" to give birth, or join gangs. We pay so much money for education, there should be armies of teachers, aides, and tutors in these schools, determined to educate these children out of poverty. Our children need to be encouraged to stay in school. They need to graduate high school with life-skills in hand. They must be prepared to enter the workforce, serve in our military, or go on to college or vocational school. Instead, our schools are filled with behavior problems and violence. And in our streets, these children, and young adults, die every day and night from gunshot wounds.

Did you connect the dots?

Be a hero. Ask, "What can I do to change this?" THINK! Are you, or your child, or your partner "caught" in the welfare trap? Are other family members and loved ones "caught" in the welfare trap? Ask, "How can I make our lives better, today?" Plan your day. Make your lives better. Strong families build strong communities. Democracy grows from the grass roots, up. Communism, Socialism, and all evil ism's rule by way of tyrants and dictators, from the top, down. Be a hero! Build yourself up. Build up your family. Build up your community. Build up your state. Call upon our 50 United States to lead the USA!

We live in dangerous times. We allowed our Federal Government to grow too large, and too powerful. The Federal Government elected to SERVE the people, now RULES the people. We created too many bureaus that cost too much money to maintain. And these bureaus have been weaponized, and used to attack the very taxpayers who pay to maintain them. Does this make sense? THINK! Ask, "How can I make America better, today?" Make a plan to "Soar With Eagles." Be a hero! At the very least, vote!

They say, "Every journey begins with the first step." And, "Today is the first day of the rest of your life." THINK! Be a Real Man. Take that first step. Be a hero! Be a Dad!